Growing Gardens

J.C Johnston

AOS Publishing, 2024

Copyright © 2024

J.C Johnston

ISBN: 978-1-990496-94-3

Cover Design: Jessica James

Visit AOS Publishing's website:
www.aospublishing.com

Table of Contents

I.
Introduction: Sowing the Seeds

imagine a place where i, the keeper of all green, listen to whispers of pain, growth, and rebirth. tend the garden, they say, but i am not human, so your language is strange to me. i hear thorns speaking of struggles, flowers blooming with triumphs, and vines twisting with the mysteries of who you are—questions of identity, all tangled in the earth.

the flora here, the fauna, they are not quiet watchers. no, they are voices, echoes of what you cannot say aloud. each leaf a memory, each petal a feeling, each drop of dew your tears or laughter, depending on how the wind blows. your gardens, i see, are not just dirt and plants. they are the very marrow of your being, a reflection of the soul you try so hard to understand.

in growing these gardens, you do not simply place roots in soil. no, you nurture yourselves, cutting away what is dead, rejoicing in what lives, always planting new seeds—of hope, of fear, of something in between. i have seen this dance for longer than you can imagine. it is a strange thing, your hands in the dirt, your heart in the sky.

so wander with me, curious one, through these tangled paths of green. here, you will find not just plants, but pieces of yourself. put on your gloves of curiosity, hold tight to your watering can of dreams. in this world that never stops growing, may you discover solace, inspiration, and the odd beauty that only something as old as time can offer.

welcome to *Growing Gardens*, where words are leaves, stanzas are branches, and poems are trees, deep-rooted in the forest of your shared experience.

II.
Seasons of Change and Transformation

Thawed Hearts in a Winter Orchard

Crisp, cold air claws at me, rooted deep in the earth's frozen
crypt
In the heart of winter's echo, where ice-beads make brittle the
boughs
Snowflakes trickle like frozen tears, crystalline tales of love
unripe
From the lonesome grey of skies they fall, burdened with
unkept vows.

In this frost-etched land, a promise twisted, a landscape scarred
Relentless winters, a push and pull of enduring and yearning.
But hear, in the quietest murmur of the subsoil, my regard,
To the marrow of these rooted bones, life's fire still burns.

Roots like gnarled fingers, clutching Earth's truths in a vice
Absorbing, pulling, drawing deep from the icy veins of winter
Their resilience, a forgotten sacrifice
In the crucible of chilling winds, love stains.

The turning of the spheres begins my transmutation,
From the cauldron of the frost-kissed earth, hope begins to
weave.
Blossom burst, verdant rush, a symphony of creation,
From a harsh winter's embrace, a canvas of relief.

In the bright glow of summer, my branches are heavy with ruby gifts
An orchard blushing with the crimson hues of perseverance
Each apple a heartbeat, a pulsing memory, an emotional burden,
Of a winter endured, a season of hurt's mitigation.

Cradled by these gnarled arms, basking in the sun's embrace
Apple-hearts hang as baubles of triumph against a toxic trace
Their sweet juice holds a story, they ripen at their own pace
A testament to growing gardens, in the harshest time and place.

With roots deep in sorrow, yet crowned with joy's array,
I stand tall, an apple tree, a keeper of the day.
In each season's passing, my truth holds sway
From pain's bitter seed, beauty finds its way.

Solstice Song

bathing in the light of the midnight sun,
chronic heat radiates relentlessly.
a shadowy companion by my side
an unending day, an eternal ache.
in the lingering solstice
i long to be blooming
amidst the icy flames.

A forest's design is akin to that of our own

Like a sapling in a dense forest
The weight of the world bears down
A delicate frame held by roots so tenuous.
With each passing day, the light dims to a frown.

A fierce storm rages within
The winds of hate and malice never cease
The weight of the downpour chokes the soul thin
And soon the sapling's spirit begins to decrease.

The once-green leaves of innocence now wilt,
Their vibrant hue fades to grey.
The trunk, a symbol of inner turmoil and guilt
With each harsh word, it sways.

The sapling dreams of being a mighty tree
But the world seems determined to keep it down.
It thinks of itself as worthless debris
If it can't please others, it's not worth the crown.

But look up to the canopy of the sky.
There, the sun shines through.
A glimmer of hope that the sapling can't deny
It's the hope that the storm will pass, and the sapling will renew.

And so, the sapling clings to the earth
Hoping to grow stronger with each passing day.
It trusts in the universe's worth
To bring it to a place where it can play.

For in this world, as in the forest
There's a place for every soul to grow
To find its light, even at its darkest
To rise up, even when it feels so low.

Embodied

i am the Northern Pike
beneath the still waters
i writhe.

a dance of silent screams
each scale, a story of unending pain.

yet in the dance,

i am alive.

Imprisoned Within a Shell

hard-shelled, I hang
between heaven and earth
bristling with potential
yet bound by my design
my seeds, yearning for the wind
my form, a prison of scales
the fall— a fearful plunge
in the tumble
comes the pain
my seeds scatter, seeking new horizons
and in their flight,
I am released.

Pain and Pleasure

a seed of doubt falls
on the vast tundra of self
lost in the frigid isolation, it
becomes a pine of understanding

there is no forest without a first tree
no self without pain.

Vibrant Squash

sprawled on the earth
I wear my stripes and warts with pride
a gourd, an outcast, a stranger
they laugh at my ungainly sprawl,
my bloated form, my distorted figure
but inside my tough rind
lies a plethora of seeds
each one a promise, a potential,
a defiance of norms and forms indeed.

so tell me,
why should my beauty fit
within the confines of their gaze
when my heart, my seeds,
are boundless worlds within?

Regrowth

in damp earth
a scent profound
whispers of the past.
fungal threads stretch
a network unseen
memories tangled, life recast.

i walk this ground
where secrets bloom,
joy breathes in the shadows.
sun peers through
a dappled gleam
forest hums, a dream untold.

mushrooms rise
a throne of ghosts
returning to love, once lost
a circle begins
laughter echoes
hearts once bound, now ash.

the fallen log
life anew,
joy we once knew fades
saplings rise
old leaves fray
growth in decay, solace found.

Spring Lakes

chilly water flows,
numbing toes, refreshing soul,
euphoric release.

Forever Spun

the circle of life spins,
turning troubles into strength
a bitter winter gives way
to the tender blush of spring
under the northern lights
we witness the dance
of joy and pain
the wild heartbeat of survival
the echo of ancestors
carried on the wind
reminding us
we are but a part of this cycle
a breath in the eternity of time

III.
Inner Strength and Resilience

Post-Traumatic Growth

the red squirrel
gathers its reserves
under the weight of winter's gaze

every acorn is a reminder
of the hard times to come,
yet it does not despair

it knows in its small heart
that the cycle of life
is about change and adaptability

Footsteps of the Moose

A moose, grand monarch of the boreal terrain
Treads through a canvas of fresh-fallen snow
Hoof-prints mark a solitary journey
Etched by the harsh winds of betrayal's blow.

Antlers adorned with frosty jewels
A crown bearing the weight of deceit.
The frigid air carries his silent sigh
Painful echoes of love's great defeat.

With every step, the echoes wane
Beneath the sky's cold, endless blue
In the heart of the wilderness, he finds solace
In each betrayal, his strength anew.

Toughened

i am the redwood—
each ring in my core
a year of weathering storms
the howling winds that tried to fell me
now whisper my name in awe
for i stand tall
proud
resilient.

Unchanged

like the arctic fox,
i changed my coat
from dark to light
to blend, to survive,

yet beneath
my heart beat the same
never fading
unchanging,

beating for what?
still, i am unsure.
but thankful i am,
all the same.

Awaken

have you ever seen
a bear after hibernation,
emerging fierce and hungry
from a den of solitude and silence?
that is me:
i sleep with my pain,
i rise with my power

Muskrat's Journey

the muskrat—the builder
surfaces from the depth
of icy blue lakes
it doesn't just survive;
it thrives—carving homes
in unforgiving terrains

i see myself in the muskrat
tearing down walls
that seek to cage my spirit,
building a refuge
from the brambles
of hateful words
i carve my space
in a world that tries to wash me away

like the muskrat,
i rise
i shape
i thrive
even when the waters
are cold and unkind.

Resilience

In the garden of innocence, a thorn did grow
A twisted vine, that shadows sow.
Its jagged barbs, a cruel embrace
Stifling the blooms in a cold, dark space.

The tender petals, once vibrant and free
Now wilted, trapped by the thorn's decree.
A grip unyielding, a poison's reign
The language of fear, and a heart's disdain.

Yet hope persists, in the garden's nook
A resilient sprout, the thorn overlooked
In the glow of compassion, a light breaks through
To banish the darkness and heal all wounds.

Grounded

the winds howl in the mountains
a mirror to the chaos within
but the caribou stands calm;
each storm shaping its sinews
into a stronger silhouette.

Unknown Strength

i am the tulip
blossoming in your garden:
bold, vibrant, tender
they ask why i don't bend
like the daisies do

i tell them
i am not made for the breeze
but for the storm.

Keep Swimming

the salmon swim upstream
a dance with death
to spawn life anew.
a journey fraught with peril
like our own voyage within
we, too, swim against the tide
to grow, to evolve
and eventually
to find our way home.

Patience's Pace

the turtle
who carries her home on her back
knows each step is victory.
her slow pace
is her strength,
not her flaw.

IV.
Nature's Teachings and Metaphors

Howling Winds

i am the wind that howls;
each gust a cry, each breeze a sigh
roaring over the Rockies
whispering tales of agony and survival
yet, in the echoes of the mountains,
i persist, i resist.

Twisting Vines

In the vast web of green
Grapevines stretch, tendrils unseen
Grasping, merging, they entwine
Silent screams are left in every wine.

Twisted tendrils, bare arms unfurl
Reaching for old roots in this twirling world.
They clutch, grasp, and enmesh
As the seasons etch their stories in flesh.

Each tendril, a crying voice
Reaching out, but not by choice.
Bound by disbelief and doubt
Their truth, society throws out.

Arms grope the vacant, absent air
Their buds linger bare.
In the curling tendrils where they were pruned
They trace the still-open wound.

Yet in unity, they grow.
Strength in numbers, they bestow.
For every tendril that's denied
A thousand more will coincide.

Growing older, leaving behind, but ever undermined
In the endless memory of the vineyard's mind.

Lessons in Ivy

Verdant heart beneath a bitter bark
Bound by fetters, stark in a forest dark.
Chains of you, chains of me,
From this pain, we long to be free.

In coiling labyrinth, we find our reign.
Woven in whispers, ivy speaks of pain.
Fingers of emerald, stretched out and thin
Wrestling with the bark's woeful skin.

Can an ivy weep, or does it bleed?
In the language of leaves, how do we read?
Tales of sorrow, of life gone awry
Silent breaths of the ivy's sigh.

Toxic, the ground where our roots unwind
The tendrils tremble, the leaves sway
Harsh are the winds that blow in our minds
In the absence of light, we try to find our way.

Through frost and drought, we've come to know
Even in shadows, ivy can grow.

No weaving of words, no testament of time
Just ivy lessons climbing in a line.
We are the ivy, the vine, the tree,
In the embrace of pain, we learn to be free.

Masked

the red fox wears a mask
in the depths of the boreal forest
a borrowed face to fool the world
that only the swaying pines
see true

Sweetgrass Stories

bent and braided,
like the sweetgrass by the creek
the whispers of my ancestors
reverberate,
telling tales
of love undefined
and identities unbound.

each plait of the sweetgrass
is a soul
twisting, bending,
embracing its own form
just as i
learn to dance with myself.

the sweetgrass and i,
we find strength
in our delicate folds,
in our willingness to bend
but never break.

A Heron's Edge

here, i stand,
a solitary sage,
lonesome heron
on the twilight's edge.
mankind declares me still,
declares me quiet
yet they know not the tempest,
that within does riot.

my keen eyes pierce
the glassy veneer of the lake,
searching for sustenance;
respite's sake.
like the mind
in melancholy's strangling grip
yearning for liberation,
for sanity's kinship.

in silence's shroud,
my turmoil's disguised.
the world sees calm
not the fear i've internalised.

thus man walks by
his demons unseen,
cloaked in normalcy's
illusive sheen.

Nature's Painful Symphony

in the vale
of crimson dusk,
i dwell—
a creature bound
by pain's fierce spell.

branches gnarled,
like bodies sick.
a willow weeps
the shadows thick.

a storm brews dark
a tempest's wail,
nature's mirror
of my travail.

torrents thrash,
a lashing rain.
echoes of
a body's aching bane.
silent, shivering,
petals close,
in fear of pain's
encroaching throes.

the moon, a sliver,
waning, pale,
like strength that fades
when illness sails.

in the fog
of suffering's haze,
i seek solace
in the sun's warm gaze—

a feeble, flickering,
distant light,
nature's promise
in my darkest night.

A Whale's Song

far from the shores
of the bustling land
in the depths of the ocean,
we make our stand.

we're humpback whales;
noble, grand,
in waters unknown
we roam unplanned.

no color
no creed
no clan
just the ebb and flow,
of life's grand plan.

beneath the waves
we understand
the ocean, our culture
our lives to command.

this is the life
we've always known.
adrift in the waters
all alone.

yet with our song,
a truth is shown
the ocean unites us
in its blue tone.

Nurture

a solitary pine stands tall
in the snow-laden North,
enduring the harsh winter.
its needles do not harden into blades
but offer shelter, warmth,
in its gentle strength, it knows
that being a protector
doesn't mean you must harm.

Silent Songs Sung

lichen cling to stone
tiny ecosystems thriving
in the cold and alone,
not demanding,
but offering
in their soft, silent hold
a rebellion
against the narrative
of powers beyond their own.

Beyond Binaries

fiddleheads, unfurling into the forest
ask not permission
to grow or change
unscripted, ungendered,
swaying in their own rhythm;
they do not play symphonies
of expected melodies
but write their own cadence.
in fernish whispers
they say,
blossom beyond binaries.

V.
The Journey of Growth and Discovery

In the Heart of the Seed

does the seed know the tree
it will become?
the seasons it will face
under the sun?
does it feel the wind's sway,
the bird's rest,
or just the pulsing self
within its chest?

roots down in darkness
branches reach for light
caught in this dance,
does the seed fear its plight?
held in the soil
is it not like our thought
bound by confusion
a fight we've fought.

but doesn't every seed grow
into tree or bloom?
through confusion
life finds room.

in the heart of a seed
a self is found
in nature's silence
wisdom is sound.

The Tree's Discovery

within the whispering forests,
i found myself
shaped by relentless winds,
bark gnarled with stories,
etched with love and pain—

bitter winters and searing summers
did not make me less,
but more:
my roots delving deeper,
my arms stretching to the sky,
strong in my solitude,
free in my existence.

Bitter Peaches

i am a peach.
soft in the Ontario sun,
my voice is the sweet juice
that drips unheeded.
they consume my flesh,
yet ignore the pit of my truth
how bitter is the seed
that is never allowed to sprout.

Different and Distinct

here in snowfall's hush
a flash of red cuts through,
noted by eyes
that find me exotic,
foreign,
my song a thread
woven in winter's stillness.

they admire my hue,
they marvel at my tune,
but few feel
the weight
of solitude.

in the echoes,
a longing
for place
among the varied,
the diverse.

each dawn,
i choose the song,
to voice what is mine,
fragile notes spun
from the heart
of the woods.

Undefined

soaring high, scanning vastness
a river of freedom
courses through my veins
an eagle am i,
defined by talons, by beak,
by penetrating gaze.
but what if i yearn
for the owl's silence
or the finch's song?
an eagle am i,
bound by nature's decree.
but who's to say
i can't have a robin's heart,
or a raven's wit,
inside an eagle's frame?

Ever Flowing

i am the lake,
still and patient,
but with rainfall and storms,
i overflow

they tell me to be still again,
to control the waters,
but
do they ever ask the sea
to tame its waves?

every ripple on my surface
is a story lived,
every dam built on my path,
a secret kept

yet
i tire of their demands,
of their accusing words
who dare tell the lake
to be a pond?
Cedar Hearts

they buried their love
in the heart of a cedar
safe from prying eyes
bark hides more than rings and time,
yet a tree knows the secret of unuttered love

Waking Blossoms

to a mind, restless,

in the quiet moments, when dusk drapes the world in soft shadows, i see you—wandering through the garden of who you are, where each step uncovers a truth, subtle and unspoken. this place, filled with the fragrances of life's many faces, whispers secrets only you can hear.

you walk between the flowers, each one a question, each petal unfolding a part of you that you've yet to fully know. the roses speak of passion, their deep red a reminder of the fire within you. the lilies, pale and serene, remind you of love's quiet strength, a love that doesn't shout but simply is.

in this garden, you realize that love isn't bound by rules or expectations. it's a dance of colors, blending, merging, becoming something new each time you look. your heart, wild and free, follows its own path, beyond the lines drawn by others, beyond even your own fears.

as you wander, know this: you're not the first to walk this path, nor will you be the last. many have sought what you seek—the freedom to love, to be, to belong. your heart is not alone in its journey. it beats in time with countless others, all searching for the same light in the twilight.

so, continue to walk, to explore, to embrace the in-between, where you truly exist. know that every step you take, every truth you uncover, brings you closer to a self that is whole, that is loved, that is free.

with all the love you deserve,

your heart, free.

Tart Berries

berries, ripe and vibrant,
hang heavy with wisdom
they don't apologise
for the space they occupy,
for their tartness or sweetness,
they simply exist
proud and unapologetic
an echo in the wild
a question to us all—
why shrink to fit
when one can grow to stand?

Wings in the Sky

The flutter of wings
Echoes through the air,
A soaring symphony
Of life and freedom.

With feathers of gold
And wings of hope,
These creatures of the sky
Are a glimpse of something more.

In watching them rise,
We see a world beyond our own,
A place where we can soar
And leave our troubles behind.

As they dip and glide
In graceful arcs of flight,
We find peace in their dance,
And our souls alight.

Though their time with us
May be all too brief,
Their spirit lives on,
A reminder of the magic
found in flight.

The Answer From Within

in silence
a lone wolf cries—
moon unmoved

years pass,
echoes of a tune unheard,
strength grows in quiet storms

no cosmic whisper,
no reply from the void
yet, in stillness, the wolf rises.

unanswered calls,
not curse, but quiet blessing
for in silence
warriors are forged.

VI.
Reflections on Life and Existence

Rooted Questions

in a forest of trees,
why must my roots be a mystery?

i am not just another tree in the forest
my rings tell a story.

a saga of growth and pain,
struggle and gain.

Hemlock's Tale

the hemlock grows
in the shadowed corners
of the thick, dense forest

so elegant, unassuming,
yet it whispers tales of sorrow,
of the poison in its veins

but it is not a poison,
not what others believe it to be
it is mistaken for another,
given a false identity

unknown are its capabilities
it is an elixir of life
waiting to be sipped, enjoyed

but the hemlock, in silence,
continues to grow
despite the rumours
in absence of belief
Fragrant Mint

breathing in the night air,
crisp like my serrated edge
the garden—my playground
a metropolis of green and bloom
each of us bestowed
a scent, a colour, a shape
yet some of us
labelled as weeds

why should my scent
be any less intoxicating,
my vigour
any less respected
than the rose's thorns
or the lily's grace?

aren't we all roots entwined
in the soil of existence,
absorbing the same sunlight,
drinking the same rain?

Falls of Voices

like the roar
of Niagara
my thoughts tumble—
crash.
powerful enough
to create energy
or destroy
from within.
everyone marvels
at the beauty
sublime, at my cascade,
but who listens
to the stories
i try to etch
in the rocks below?

Skittering to a Halt

field mice skittering in the wheat
so small, so quick
invisible 'till the harvest

i was once like them,
running through life
faster than the wind
but now my legs don't carry me
like they used to

still, i remember the grain,
the thrill of the chase,
the joy in every breath,
and i gather strength
from the tiny hearts
beating in the field

Flying

i am the Canada goose
flying south for winter
i carry the ache in my wings
but it does not weigh me down
maybe it's spite, maybe strength
it fuels me
each flap
echoes my perseverance

Cries in the night

how much like the loon am i,
crying in the night
its haunting melody
an echo of my plight.
my song is lost
beneath the waves
of their cruel words
and rigorous maze.
the moon's reflection
on the tranquil lake
a mirror to my soul
reveals the heartache.

Chamomile Pleas

a carpet of tiny suns
in a sea of green
perfume, serenity
caresses the breeze

they say i'm common
too pale
a wallflower
lost
in the garden's grand scheme

they do not see
my growth,
do not feel
my calming
embrace

each petal, each leaf
holds a tale
of roots planted in foreign soil
silent endurance,
quiet strength
whispered only to the moon
and the stars

like dawn breaking
the darkest night
i bloom
undeterred
my spirit
unfettered

in this strange land
i've made my home

Broken Dams

i, the diligent beaver,
work under the quiet moon
constructing dreams of timber and mud
yet when morning comes,
they doubt the strength of my dam
my nocturnal toil unseen
my persistence unacknowledged.

Stung

the pain
is a stinging nettle's kiss
hidden amidst the fern's embrace
it swells, it throbs,
blossoming like a prickly bud,
a voice in verdant flood
a lover's touch, once sought, now missed,
pierces deep, a nettle's tryst.

Hiking

mountaintop silence,
only wind and birdsong heard,
a spirit takes flight.

Fluid

lake stilled at dawn,
its mirror surface
holds not vanity
but a lesson,
all can see themselves
in its depths

fluid, ever-changing,
like the silver mirrored dawn,
in ripples and currents,
in the ebb and flow,
is the dance we know.

in the water's kiss,
in the cool morning's bliss,
an echo of the universe,
whispering this:

"who you are
is not set in stone.
your essence, your core,
is yours to own.
fluid as water,
your nature can alter,
be it body, belief,
or the love you offer."

Decay

i am the tree,
fallen over and forgotten,
a decaying log
left alone to decompose

my body
their nourishment,
into the earth
i slowly dissolve

i am both enriching
and being drained
they feed from me
take from my soul

i am dying
in order to keep
everyone around me
alive.

Eyes of the Land

we are the mountain stream:
quiet, serene, a dream
we watch your tears spill
and echo them, hushed and still

the wise old owl in the tree
sees your pain, quiet as can be
he hoots at the moon, so high
teaching us it's okay to cry.

we are the northern lights:
waltzing through endless nights
we see your pain, your strife,
and dance to the rhythm of life

we are the pines standing tall:
through harsh winters and fall
we watch you bear your load
and learn to endure the cold

we are the eyes of the land:
forever watchful, steadfast guardians stand
your cries, your sorrows, they reach our core
your breath and soul, they do implore

they echo through the ancient wind,
ripple across waters, yet to be pinned,
whisper through the leafy veil,
resonate in the coyote's wail.

unseen, unheard, we are always near,
in every whispering wind, every dewdrop clear.
we exist, we thrive, we watch, we see,
in our silent vigil forever we'll be.

Songs of Solitude

like the wolf who howls to the moon,
i, too, shout into the void
embracing my solitude
for in the echo
i hear my own voice
calling back to me

Gazing Upwards

golden beams of light
a divine sight in the sky
a glimpse of heaven

Furled Wings

a monarch rests on a milkweed stem
a journey behind, a journey ahead
no one sees the tiger within
that roars in silence
fearing the din

it longs to flaunt its stripes,
yet hides beneath
a symphony of orange kites

if only it could spread its wings,
show the world
the truth of things

yet till then, it quietly sings
a muted song
of hidden kings

The Corn's Advice

in the field, i stand tall
children of the sun, children of the earth
an army of golden sceptres,
each of us adorned
in layers of silk and mystery

is it not peculiar
that they call us male and female?

silk tassels dancing with the wind,
bodies hidden beneath a shroud,
as if nature, too,
is confined by these names

but the wind knows
as it plays among us
that we are not our tassels,
nor our bodies, nor our silk,
but children of the sun, children of the earth,
each kernel of our being
swaying in life's breeze.

Life's Changes

upon this land
i learned how to bear the world,
but the once-nimble steps
are now slow and deliberate
there's a new rhythm to life
redefining what was once swift,
yet with each heavy breath,
i adjust and shift

VII.
Conclusion: Tending the garden

i am the land, ageless, bountiful, a silent custodian of time's untamed garden. for centuries, i have cradled the roots of existence, tended to the sprouts of human lives unfurling in my soil. through the eyes of my children—the ancient oak, the gentle daisy, the vigilant pine—i have witnessed the mosaic of your stories, the intertwining of pain, pleasure, the blooming of identities as diverse as wildflowers gracing my meadows.

in the whispers of leaves, i've heard your joys, sorrows. rustling grass has carried your secrets, rivers have washed away your tears. i've seen love take root, a steadfast sprout in the earth, and heartache wither, autumn's last petal. i've sheltered tender saplings of new beginnings, stood by crumbling bark of final goodbyes.

my gardens have flourished with your laughter, wilted beneath the weight of your despair. yet, even in the harshest winters, i have waited—patient, unwavering—for the thaw that heralds your return to my embrace.

as the seasons wheel overhead, as the stars gaze down upon us, i am here, tending to the garden of life, nurturing each soul-seed with a gardener's solemn vow: to witness, to cherish, to endure. for in the end, we are all but flowers in the eternal garden, blooming brilliantly before returning to the earth from which we came.